Common Core Lessons & Activities:

Key Events of World War II

By Carole Marsh

Published by Gallopade International, Inc.

Printed in the U.S.A. (Peachtree City, Georgia)

TABLE OF CONTENTS

G: Includes Graphic Organizer
GO: Graphic Organizer is also available 8½" x
download at www.gallopade.com/client/(
(numbers above correspond to the graphic organ

I0895169

World War II Begins

Read the text and answer the questions.

The events leading to World War II began in 1919 with the Treaty of Versailles at the end of World War I. The Treaty of Versailles demanded that Germany pay reparations to the Allies for causing most of the destruction of World War I. In addition, Germany was forced to give up much of its military, weapons, and land. After World War I, Germany had many economic and political problems.

In 1933, Adolf Hitler and the Nazi Party took power in Germany. Hitler was a strong leader and convinced the German people that he could make Germany a powerful country again. Hitler began to rebuild the German military. In 1938, Germany invaded Austria and part of Czechoslovakia, the Sudetenland, in 1939.

In order to avoid another world war, Great Britain and France signed an appeasement plan called the Munich Pact with Germany. In the agreement, Hitler promised he would not invade any other territories.

On September 1, 1939, Hitler broke his promise when Germany invaded Poland. As a result, Great Britain and France declared war on Germany. Soon afterward, Germany's allies declared war on Great Britain and France. World War II had begun!

1. A. Use a dictionary to define reparations as it is used in the text.
   B. Why was Germany required to pay reparations?
2. A. Use a dictionary to define appeasement as it is used in the text.
   B. What was the purpose of the appeasement plan? Did it succeed?
3. Based on the text, why did Hitler rebuild Germany's military? Cite evidence from the text to support your answer.
4. What does it mean to "declare war"? Why did Great Britain and France declare war on Germany? Explain.
5. Explain the cause and effect relationship between the Treaty of Versailles in 1919 and Hitler's rise to power in 1933.

PRIMARY SOURCE ANALYSIS

Chamberlain's Speech

Read the text and answer the questions.

Excerpt from Neville Chamberlain's Declaration of War to Great Britain
Sept. 3, 1939 at 11:15 a.m.

This morning the British Ambassador in Berlin handed the German Government a final Note stating that, unless we heard from them by 11 o'clock that they were prepared at once to withdraw their troops from Poland, a state of war would exist between us.

I have to tell you now that no such undertaking has been received, and that consequently this country is at war with Germany.

You can imagine what a bitter blow it is to me that all my long struggle to win peace has failed. Yet I cannot believe that there is anything more or anything different that I could have done and that would have been more successful.

Up to the very last it would have been quite possible to have arranged a peaceful and honourable settlement between Germany and Poland, but Hitler would not have it...

We and France are today...going to the aid of Poland...We have done all that any country could do to establish peace...

1. What is the purpose of Chamberlain's speech?
2. Describe the tone of Chamberlain's speech. What words and phrases help create the tone?
3. What German actions caused Chamberlain to give this speech?
4. Who does Chamberlain blame for the start of World War II? Cite evidence from the text to support your answer.
5. Is the phrase "bitter blow" figurative or literal? Explain.
6. What is the **most significant** fact communicated in the text?
7. What countries are involved in the conflict described in Chamberlain's speech?

MAIN IDEA ORGANIZER

Leaders of World War II

Use a classroom or online resource to research the major leaders of World War II. Complete the organizer by identifying each leader as either an Allied leader or an Axis leader and describe the roles of each in World War II.

Adolf Hitler

Franklin D. Roosevelt

Benito Mussolini

LEADERS OF WW II

Emperor Hirihito

Joseph Stalin

Harry S. Truman

Winston Churchill

Axis-Occupied Europe

Analyze the map and answer the questions.

Axis-Occupied Europe — September, 1942

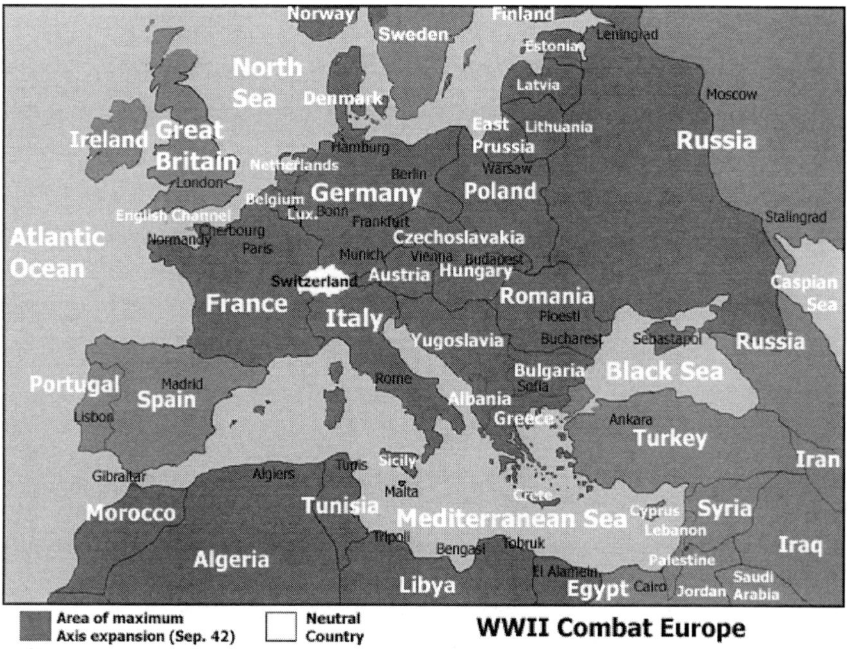

Courtesy of Wikipedia

1. A. What information does this map provide?
   B. What is represented by the darkest area?
   C. What is represented by the lightest area?
2. Approximately how many countries did the Axis Powers occupy in 1942?
3. Russia was an Allied country, not an Axis Power. Explain why part of Russia is darkened by the Axis color.
4. Use the map to explain how geography helped Great Britain in WWII.
5. Based on the map, explain why World War II is called a "World War."

BONUS: What Axis Power and Allied country are not included on this map?

World War II Vocabulary

Use a dictionary and other resources to complete the graphic organizer for each vocabulary word.

alliance	blitzkrieg	rationing
Allies	concentration camp	reparations
appeasement	D-Day	United Nations
atomic bomb	Holocaust	VE Day
Axis Powers	kamikaze	VJ Day

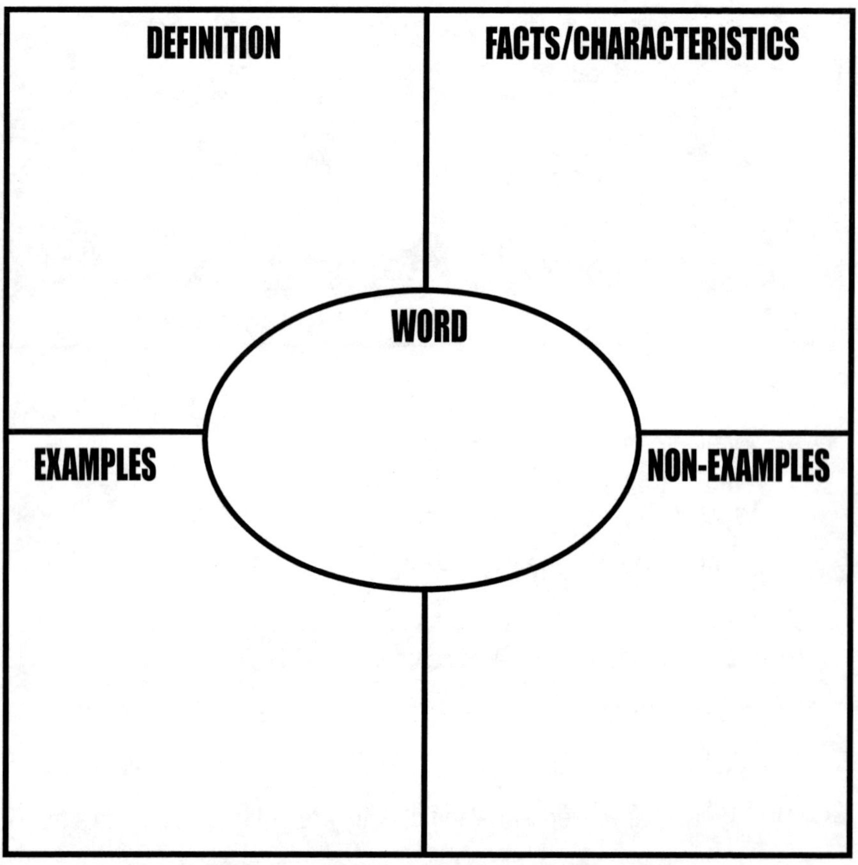

PRIMARY SOURCE ANALYSIS

Attack on Pearl Harbor

This photograph was taken from the Ford Island seaplane base December 7, 1941, during the Japanese military bombing of the U.S. naval base in Pearl Harbor, Hawaii.

Look at the photograph and answer the questions.

Courtesy of Wikimedia Commons

1. What do you notice first? Why? Make 3-5 other observations.
2. Write a title for this photograph to express the main idea.
3. Describe the tone of this photograph. How do light and dark elements affect the tone?
4. What inferences can you make about the men in the foreground of the photograph? Explain.
5. Write a short fictional narrative from the perspective of an American sailor during the Attack on Pearl Harbor. Describe what you see, hear, smell, and feel. Proofread and edit your work.

PRIMARY SOURCE ANALYSIS

Day in Infamy Speech

Read the text and answer the questions.

Address Delivered by President Franklin D. Roosevelt to the Congress

By: President Franklin D. Roosevelt

December 8, 1941 (excerpt)

Yesterday, December 7, 1941—a date which will live in infamy—the United States of America was suddenly and deliberately attacked by naval and air forces of the Empire of Japan...

It will be recorded that the distance of Hawaii from Japan makes it obvious that the attack was deliberately planned many days or even weeks ago. During the intervening time the Japanese Government has deliberately sought to deceive the United States by false statements and expressions of hope for continued peace.

The attack yesterday on the Hawaiian Islands has caused severe damage to American naval and military forces. Very many American lives have been lost...

The facts of yesterday speak for themselves. The people of the United States have already formed their opinions and well understand the implications to the very life and safety of our Nation.

As Commander in Chief of the Army and Navy I have directed that all measures be taken for our defense.

Always will we remember the character of the onslaught against us.

No matter how long it may take us to overcome this premeditated invasion, the American people in their righteous might will win through to absolute victory...

Hostilities exist. There is no blinking at the fact that our people, our territory, and our interests are in grave danger.

With confidence in our armed forces—with the unbounded determination of our people—we will gain the inevitable triumph—so help us God.

I ask that the Congress declare that since the unprovoked and dastardly attack by Japan on Sunday, December 7, a state of war has existed between the United States and the Japanese Empire.

PART A: Use the text to determine whether each statement is **true** or **false**.

1. ______ Before December 7, 1941, the United States Military was not directly involved in World War II.
2. ______ The Japanese accidentally bombed Pearl Harbor.
3. ______ No Americans died in the Pearl Harbor Attack.
4. ______ The Japanese government lied about wanting to maintain peace with the U.S.

PART B: Use the text to identify what is being described.

5. "onslaught" "invasion" "unprovoked and dastardly attack"
6. "Commander in Chief of the Army and Navy"
7. "a date which will live in infamy"
8. "state of war"

PART C: Make inferences from the text to answer the questions.

9. A. Use a dictionary to define <u>infamy</u>.
   B. What does Roosevelt mean by the phrase "a date which will live in infamy"?
   C. Was he correct?
10. Explain the historical context of the address. What is Franklin D. Roosevelt's purpose for writing this address?
11. What evidence does Roosevelt give to conclude that the attack was deliberate?
12. Use the text to make three inferences about Franklin Delano Roosevelt's leadership as president.
13. According to the address, how has attack affected the American people?
14. Use evidence from the text to explain the relationship between the attack on Pearl Harbor and the United States' involvement in WWII.

BONUS: Why was this address given to Congress?

Rationing in the U.S.

Use online and classroom resources to complete the graphic organizer with the problems, solutions, and effects of rationing in the U.S. during World War II.

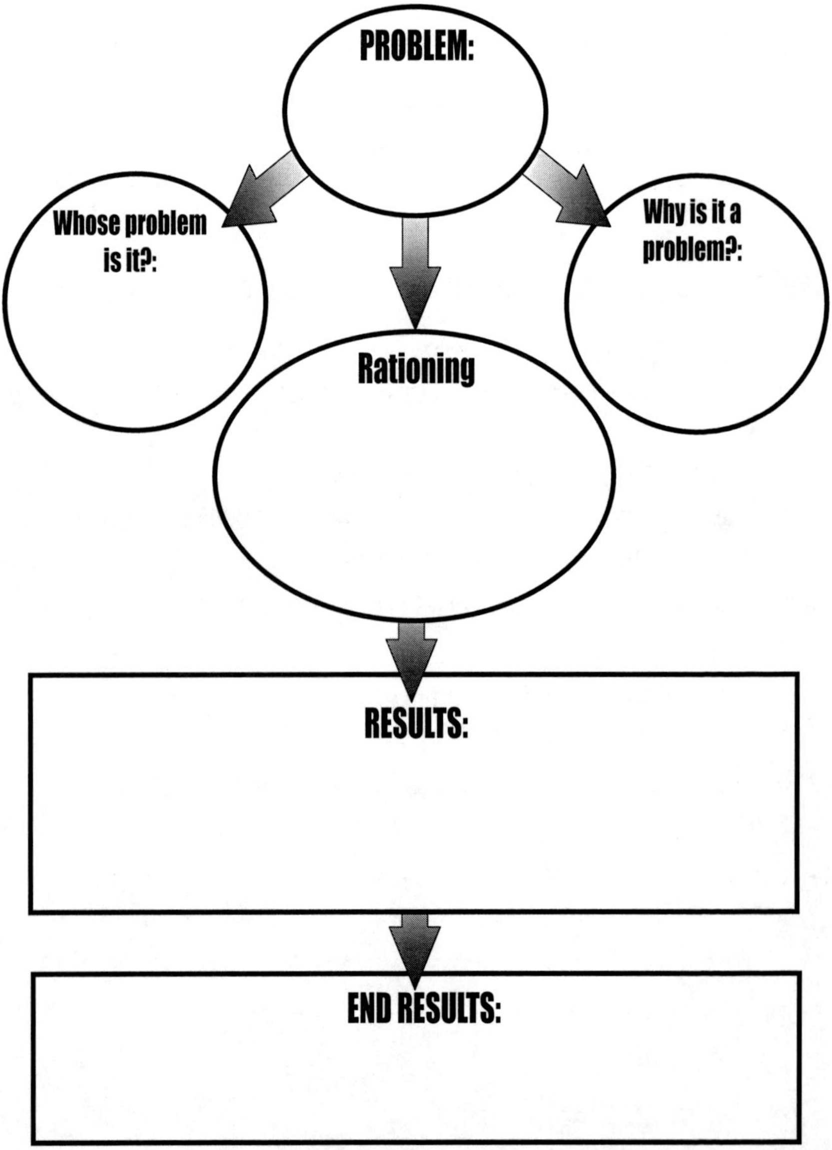

PRIMARY SOURCE ANALYSIS

Dig on for Victory

Look at the poster and answer the questions.

Courtesy of Wikipedia

1. Who is the intended audience of this poster?
2. What is the purpose of this poster?
3. What is meant by the phrase "DIG ON"? Why might this phrase have been chosen?
4. What is meant by the word "VICTORY"? Explain.
5. A. How is this illustration effective? Cite evidence.
   B. Is this illustration effective to all audiences? Explain.

World War II

Complete the graphic organizer with key causes, events, and effects of World War II.

Causes:

Events:

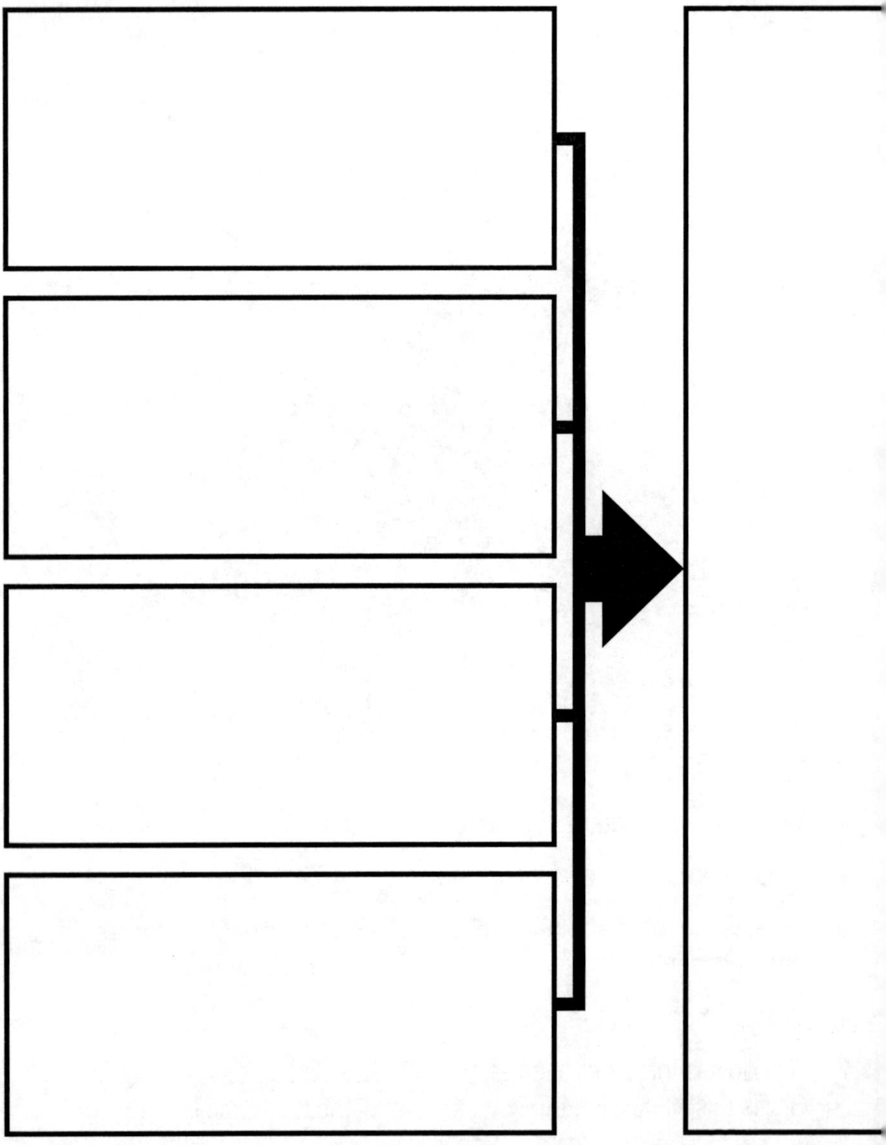

Effects:

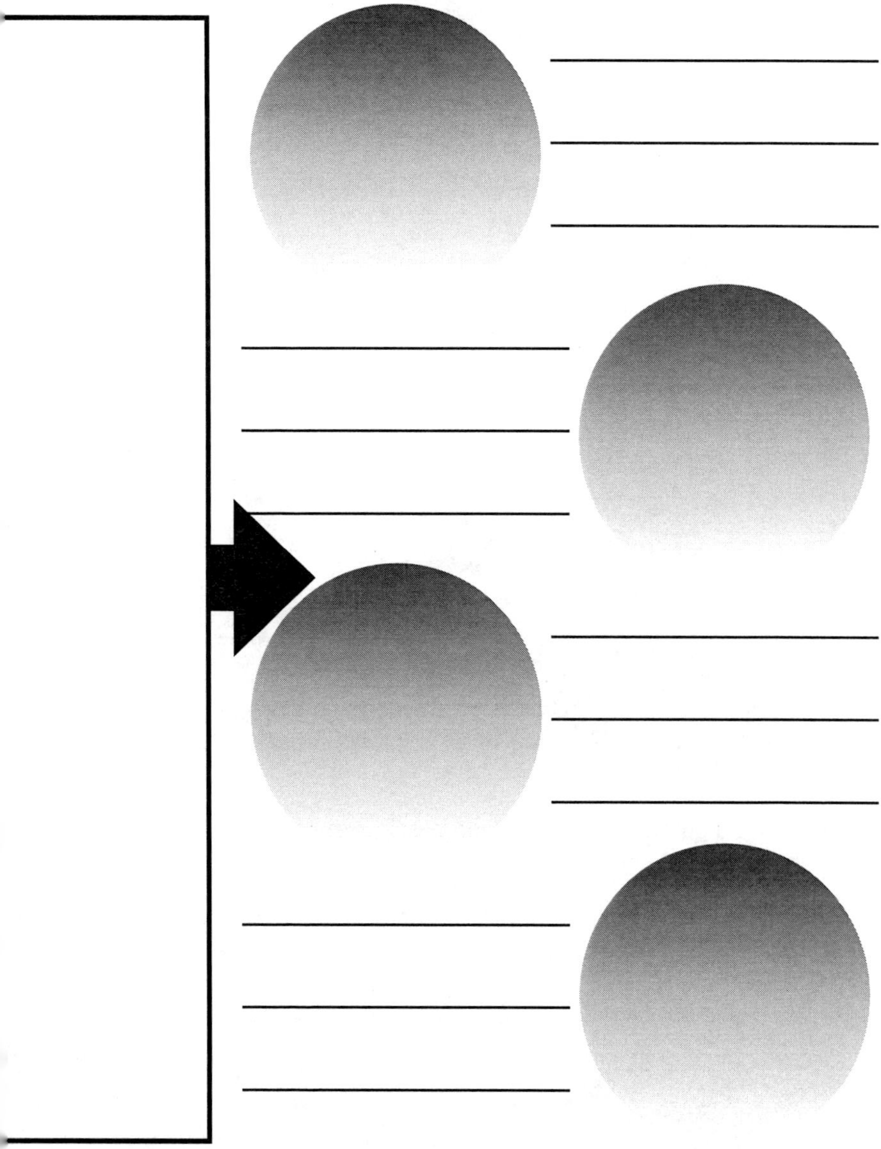

PRIMARY SOURCE ANALYSIS

Rosie the Riveter

Look at the poster and answer the questions.

Courtesy of Wikipedia

1. Explain the purpose of the message at the top of the poster. Who is the intended audience? What does it mean?
2. A. Make 3-5 inferences about the poster's depiction of women.
   B. What is the artist's purpose for drawing Rosie like this?
3. In your opinion, is this poster effective? Why or why not?
4. Use an online or classroom resource to make a list of jobs women did during World War II. Share your lists with the class.

Tuskegee Airmen

Read the text and answer the questions.

In World War I, no African Americans were allowed to be pilots in the U.S. Armed Forces. Over two decades later in World War II, the Tuskegee Airmen were the first African American pilots in the United States Armed Forces.

The Tuskegee Airmen get their name from the aviation training facility at Tuskegee Institute in Alabama. However, the "Tuskegee Airmen" are not just pilots. The group includes all the members of the African American aviation division—pilots, navigators, bombardiers, support staff, and all the instructors at Tuskegee Institute.

During World War II, African Americans experienced racial segregation in many forms. The U.S. military was still segregated, and the Tuskegee Airmen faced discrimination and unfair treatment at home and in the military. The U.S. military claimed the Tuskegee Airmen were "separate but equal," but the Airmen were trained in cramped classrooms and faced disrespect from white troops and commanders. They were not allowed to fly with white pilots and received less public recognition for their efforts.

Nevertheless, the Tuskegee Airmen became a well-respected airborne squadron. These highly trained men flew beside bombers as protection against enemy fighters. The Airmen were so successful that bombers nicknamed the Airmen the "Red Tail Angels" because of their planes' red-painted tails. Their efforts during World War II challenged racism in the military and proved that African Americans could perform to the highest standards.

1. A. Define discrimination as it is used in the text.
   B. How did discrimination affect African Americans in the United States military?
2. What can you infer about the Tuskegee Airmen from their nickname "Red Tail Angels?"
3. In what ways did the Tuskegee Airmen overcome racism?
4. Write a journal entry from the perspective of a Tuskegee Airman describing your feelings toward "separate but equal" in the military.

PRIMARY SOURCE ANALYSIS

D-Day

On June 6, 1944, Allied troops invaded Nazi-controlled Normandy, France. This photograph is a scene from the invasion and is famously called "Into the Jaws of Death".

Analyze the photograph and answer the questions.

Courtesy of the National Archives

1. Make 3-5 inferences from the photograph about the conditions soldiers experienced in the D-Day invasion
2. Describe the mood of this photograph. What details contribute to the mood?
3. A. Why do you think this photograph is called "Into the Jaws of Death"?
   B. What does this phrase tell you about the D-Day invasion?
4. Use an online resource to research the results of the D-Day Invasion. In a well-organized essay, write your response to the question "Was the D-Day invasion successful?" Proofread and edit your work.

PRIMARY SOURCE ANALYSIS

Iwo Jima

From February 19, 1945 to March 26, 1945, United States Armed Forces invaded the island of Iwo Jima, Japan where they fought the Japanese military. This photograph depicts five Marines and a Navy corpsman raising the flag of the United States atop Mount Suribachi on the island of Iwo Jima.

Analyze the photograph and answer the questions.

Courtesy of the National Archives

1. What is the mood of this photograph? Cite details from the photograph to explain your answer.
2. Which details from the photograph best support the idea of "patriotism"?
3. What inferences can you make about the Battle of Iwo Jima?
4. What is the purpose of raising a U.S. flag on Iwo Jima?
5. Write a title for the photograph that characterizes the people or the event.

The Holocaust

Read the text and answer the questions.

The Holocaust was the genocide of approximately 11 million people by the German Nazi Party. Most notably, the Nazi Party targeted the Jewish people based upon their cultural heritage. This mass murder saw the death of approximately 6 million Jews. The Nazis also killed German Gypsies, Polish people, Slavic people, homosexuals, and political enemies of the Germans.

Before WWII, Hitler and the Nazi Party blamed the Jewish people for Germany's economic problems. The Nazi Party passed laws discriminating against Jews living in Germany. They took away Jewish businesses and banned Jews from public schools, libraries, and hospitals. Hitler and the Nazi Party believed that the German, "Aryan," race was a superior race to all others. To strengthen Germany and conquer Europe in WWII, the Nazis sought to destroy all people they considered inferior, especially the Jewish people. They called Hitler's plan the "Final Solution."

In 1942, German soldiers loaded millions of people (Jewish, Polish, Slavic, etc.) into trains and sent them to concentration camps. The Nazis built nearly 1,500 concentration camps across Europe. Prisoners in these camps faced squalid living conditions, starvation, brutal physical labor, and disease. Camps such as Auschwitz and Treblinka were known as extermination camps or "death camps." These camps were designed for the purpose of killing prisoners by gas or overwork. By the end of 1942, more than 4 million Jews had been killed.

1. A. Use a dictionary to write a definition of genocide.
   B. In what ways was the Holocaust a genocide?
2. Write an appropriate title for each paragraph.
3. According to the Nazis, what problems did Hitler's "Final Solution" try to resolve? How did the "Final Solution" affect the Jewish people?
4. What was the purpose of the German concentration camps in WWII?
5. In a well-organized response, use evidence from the text to support Elie Wiesel's famous quote, "While not all victims were Jews, all Jews were victims." Proofread and edit your work.

United Nations

Use an online or classroom resource to research the relationship between the League of Nations and the United Nations.

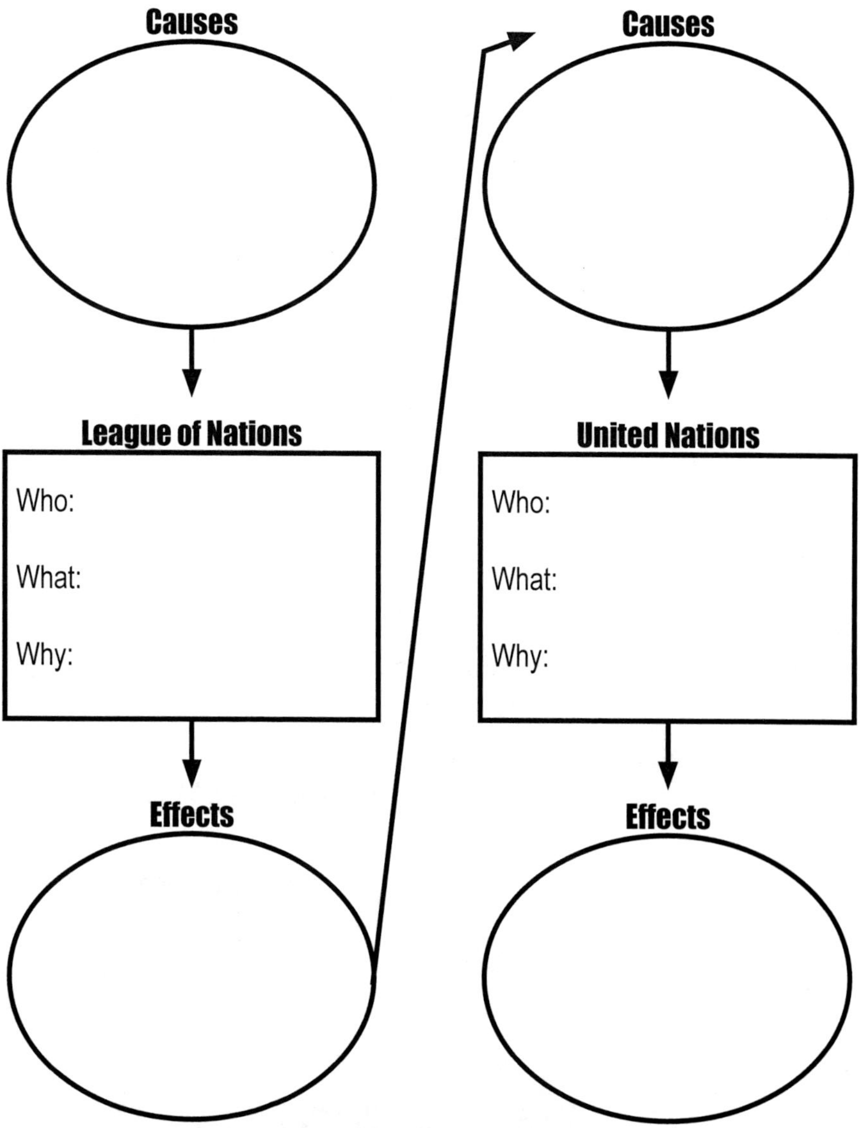

VE & VJ Day

Read the text and answer the questions.

World War II was a global war that began in 1939 and ended in 1945. The end of World War II brought mixed emotions to the world. People were saddened by all the lives lost, but relieved that the war was finally over. Two important days mark the end of World War II—VE Day in Europe and VJ Day in Japan.

On May 8, 1945 Germany surrendered to the Allies. This day is referred to as "VE Day," which stands for "Victory in Europe." This day officially marks the date when the Allies formally accepted the unconditional surrender of the armed forces of Nazi Germany.

The United States and the other Allied countries were happy the war was over in Europe; however, fighting against Japan still raged on in the Pacific. As a step to end the war with Japan, the United States issued the Potsdam Declaration on July 26, 1945. The Potsdam Declaration ordered the Japanese to surrender, or else Japan would face "prompt and utter destruction."

Unfortunately, the Japanese did not surrender. The United States responded by dropping atomic bombs on Hiroshima and Nagasaki—two major cities in Japan. Japan finally surrendered on August 14, 1945. It was not until September 2, 1945 that a formal surrender ceremony occurred in Tokyo Bay, Japan aboard the battleship *USS Missouri*. September 2 is celebrated as "VJ Day," which stands for "Victory over Japan."

1. Identify the importance of VE Day and VJ Day. What is the difference between these days? How are they connected?
2. A. Why was the Potsdam Declaration issued?
   B. What was the purpose of using the phrase "prompt and utter destruction"?
3. Based on the date the Potsdam Declaration was issued and the date Japan surrendered, what can you infer about the atomic bomb?
4. Predict what might have happened had the atomic bombs not been dropped on Japan.

Key Events of World War II

Put these events in chronological order in the graphic organizer.

U.S. drops atomic bomb on Hiroshima	D-Day Invasion	VE Day	Germany invades Poland	Battle of Iwo Jima
United Nations is created	Japanese attack Pearl Harbor	Great Britain & France declare war on Germany	U.S. drops atomic bomb on Nagasaki	VJ Day

World War II Events:

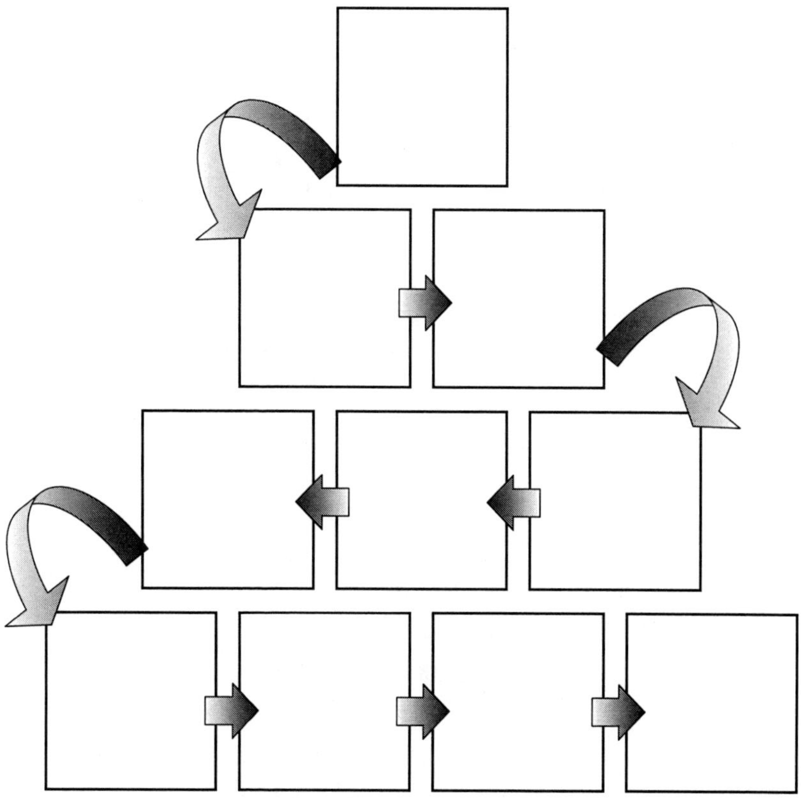

Atomic Bomb Decision

After the United States issued the Potsdam Declaration on July 26, 1945, Japan did not surrender. As a result, the United States dropped an atomic bomb called "Little Boy" on Hiroshima on August 6th and "Fat Man" on Nagasaki on August 9th. Before the dropping of the atomic bombs, much discussion and debate took place with President Harry S. Truman. These letters are examples of correspondence between the American people and President Truman.

Read the letters and answer the questions.

Telegram from Federal Council of the Churches of Christ in America

By: Samuel M. Cavert, General Secretary
August 9, 1945, Received at 11:22 a.m.

Honorable Harry S Truman,

Many Christians deeply disturbed over use of atomic bombs against Japanese cities because of their necessarily indiscriminate destructive efforts and because their use sets extremely dangerous precedent for the future of mankind. Bishop Oxnam, President of the Council, and John Foster Dulles, Chairman, of its commission on a just a durable peace are preparing statement for probable release tomorrow urging that atomic bombs be regarded as trust for humanity and that Japanese nation be given genuine opportunity and time to verify facts about new bomb and to accept surrender terms. Respectfully urge that ample opportunity be given Japan to reconsider ultimatum before any further devastation by atomic bomb is visited upon her people.

Federal Council of the Churches of Christ in America

Samuel M. Cavert, General Secretary

Letter from President Harry S. Truman to Samuel M. Cavert

By: President Harry S. Truman
August 11, 1945

My dear Mr. Cavert:

I appreciated very much your telegram of August ninth.

Nobody is more disturbed over the use of Atomic bombs than I am but I was greatly disturbed over the unwarranted attack by the Japanese on Pearl Harbor and their murder of our prisoners of war. The only language they seem to understand is the one we have been using to bombard them.

When you have to deal with a beast you have to treat him as a beast. It is most regrettable but nevertheless true.

Sincerely yours,

Harry S. Truman

1. Explain the purpose of each letter.
2. What words or phrases in the first letter reveal Samuel Cavert's opinion of using the atomic bomb?
3. What does Samuel Cavert ask President Truman to consider? Why?
4. Use the first letter to make a short list of reasons why Truman should NOT have used an atomic bomb against Japan.
5. How does President Truman feel about using the atomic bomb? Cite evidence from the second letter to support your response.
6. What is President Truman's opinion of the Japanese military? What words and phrases in the second letter reveal his opinion?
7. Do you agree or disagree with President Truman's decision to drop the atomic bombs? Write a letter to President Truman expressing your opinion. Provide a convincing argument.

Correlations to Common Core State Standards

For your convenience, correlations are listed page-by-page and for the entire book!

This book is correlated to the Common Core State Standards for English Language Arts grades 3-8, and to Common Core State Standards for Literacy in History, Science, & Technological Subjects grades 6-8.

Correlations are highlighted in gray.

	READING	WRITING	LANGUAGE	SPEAKING & LISTENING
	Includes: RI: Reading Informational Text; RH: Reading History	*Includes:* W: Writing; WHST: Writing History, Science, & Technology	*Includes:* L: Language; LF: Language Foundational Skills	*Includes:* SL: Speaking & Listening
PAGE #	RI / RH	W / WHST	L / LF	SL
2	**1 2** 3 **4 5** 6 7 8 9 **10**	**1** 2 3 4 5 6 7 8 9 10	1 2 3 **4** 5 **6**	1 2 3 4 5 6
3	**1 2 3** 4 5 **6** 7 8 9 **10**	**1** 2 3 4 5 6 7 8 9 10	1 2 3 4 **5 6**	1 2 3 4 5 6
4	1 2 3 4 5 6 7 8 **9 10**	1 2 3 4 5 **6 7 8 9 10**	1 2 3 4 5 6	1 2 3 4 5 6
5	1 2 3 4 5 6 **7** 8 9 **10**	1 2 3 4 5 6 7 8 9 10	1 2 3 4 5 6	1 2 3 4 5 6
6	1 2 3 **4** 5 6 7 8 9 **10**	1 2 3 4 5 6 7 8 9 10	1 2 3 **4** 5 **6**	1 2 3 4 5 6
7	1 2 3 4 5 6 **7** 8 9 **10**	1 2 **3 4 5** 6 7 8 9 **10**	1 2 3 4 5 6	1 2 3 4 5 6
8-9	**1 2** 3 **4** 5 6 7 **8** 9 **10**	**1 2** 3 4 5 6 7 8 9 10	1 2 3 **4 5 6**	1 2 3 4 5 6
10	1 2 3 4 **5** 6 7 8 **9 10**	1 2 3 4 5 6 **7 8 9 10**	1 2 3 4 5 6	1 2 3 4 5 6
11	1 2 3 4 5 6 **7** 8 9 **10**	1 2 3 4 5 6 7 8 9 10	1 2 3 4 **5 6**	1 2 3 4 5 6
12-13	1 2 **3** 4 **5** 6 7 8 9 **10**	1 2 3 4 5 6 7 8 9 10	1 2 3 4 5 6	1 2 3 4 5 6
14	1 2 3 4 5 **6 7** 8 9 **10**	1 2 3 **4** 5 6 **7 8 9 10**	1 2 3 4 5 6	**1** 2 3 **4** 5 **6**
15	**1 2** 3 **4** 5 6 7 8 9 **10**	**1** 2 **3** 4 5 6 7 8 9 **10**	1 2 3 **4** 5 **6**	1 2 3 4 5 6
16	1 2 3 4 5 6 **7** 8 9 **10**	**1 2** 3 **4 5** 6 **7 8 9 10**	1 2 3 4 5 6	1 2 3 4 5 6
17	1 2 3 4 5 6 **7** 8 9 **10**	1 2 3 **4** 5 6 7 8 9 **10**	1 2 3 4 5 6	1 2 3 4 5 6
18	**1 2** 3 **4** 5 6 7 8 9 **10**	1 2 **3 4** 5 6 7 8 9 **10**	1 2 3 4 5 6	1 2 3 4 5 6
19	1 2 3 4 **5** 6 7 8 9 **10**	1 2 3 4 5 6 **7 8 9 10**	1 2 3 4 5 6	1 2 3 4 5 6
20	**1 2** 3 4 **5** 6 7 8 9 **10**	1 2 3 4 5 6 7 8 9 10	1 2 3 **4** 5 **6**	1 2 3 4 5 6
21	1 2 3 4 **5** 6 7 8 9 **10**	1 2 3 4 5 6 7 8 9 10	1 2 3 4 5 6	1 2 3 4 5 6
22-23	**1 2** 3 4 **5** 6 7 **8** 9 **10**	**1** 2 3 **4** 5 6 7 8 9 **10**	1 2 3 4 5 6	1 2 3 4 5 6
COMPLETE BOOK	**1 2 3 4 5 6 7 8 9 10**	**1 2 3 4 5 6 7 8 9 10**	1 2 3 **4 5 6**	**1** 2 3 **4** 5 **6**

For the complete Common Core standard identifier, combine your grade + "." + letter code above + "." + number code above.

In addition to the correlations indicated here, the activities may be adapted or expanded to align to additional standards and to meet the diverse needs of your unique students!